THE TRINITARIAN CONTROVERSY

IN THE FOURTH CENTURY

THE TRINITARIAN CONTROVERSY
IN THE FOURTH CENTURY

BY DAVID BERNARD

The Trinitarian Controversy In the Fourth Century

by David K. Bernard

©1993, David K. Bernard
Printing History: 1996

Cover Design by Tim Agnew

Printed in United States of America

Library of Congress Cataloging-in-Publication Data

Bernard, David K., 1956-
    The trinitarian controversy in the fourth century / by David K. Bernard.
        p.   cm.
    Sequel to: Oneness and Trinity, A.D. 100-200.
    Includes bibliographical references and index.
    ISBN 1-56722-009-6
    1. Trinity—History of doctrines—Early church, ca. 30-600.
2. Trinity—Controversial literature. 3. Oneness doctrine
(Pentecostalism) I. Title.
BT109.B47   1993
231'.004'09015— dc20   93-16363
                                                        CIP

Contents

Preface

This book discusses the doctrine of God in Christendom during the fourth century A.D. It has two main purposes: (1) to trace the development of trinitarianism and (2) to find and evaluate evidence for Oneness beliefs during this time.

The Trinitarian Controversy in the Fourth Century is a sequel to *Oneness and Trinity, A.D. 100-300* by David K. Bernard, which Word Aflame Press published in 1991. It relies upon the evidence in that book regarding the doctrinal beliefs and developments of the second and third centuries. (See chapter 11 of *Oneness and Trinity* for conclusions.) It also presumes that the reader understands the Oneness doctrine and how it differs from trinitarianism. (For a discussion, see chapter 1 of *Oneness and Trinity*. For a full biblical treatment, see *The Oneness of God* by David K. Bernard.)

This book is an expansion of a paper given at the 1992 Symposium on Oneness Pentecostalism on January 9, 1992, in St. Louis, Missouri, entitled "From Nicea to Constantinople: The Trinitarian Controversy in the Fourth Century." Because of the nature of the subject matter and the original forum of its presentation, some of the terms in this book are technical and specialized. To assist the reader's understanding, a glossary has been included.

History cannot alter or replace biblical truth, nor can it establish or repudiate apostolic doctrine. The clear teaching of Scripture must be the only basis of our belief and practice. My hope is that this historical investigation will help the reader to brush past nonbiblical tradition and see the Word of God more clearly.

1

The Road to Nicea

In the Old Catholic Age (c. A.D. 170 to 325), Christendom shifted from the biblical belief in one God toward a form of trinitarianism.[1] The trinitarians of that age divided the personality of God in tritheistic fashion, and they denied the full deity of Jesus Christ by subordinating the second person of their trinity to the first person.[2]

By 300, some form of trinitarianism and trinitarian baptism had become dominant in Christendom, but orthodox trinitarianism as we know it today had yet to be formulated clearly or established solidly. We will discuss how such a formulation occurred in the fourth century, focusing particularly on the two ecumenical councils crucial to this process: the Council of Nicea in A.D. 325 and the Council of Constantinople in A.D. 381.

In the second and third centuries most Christians affirmed the absolute oneness of God and the full deity of Jesus Christ and did not think in trinitarian categories.[3] We can label this belief generically by the term *modalism*. The most prominent teacher of modalism in the third century was Sabellius, who held that Father, Son, and Holy Spirit were modes (designations, manifestations, not persons) of the one God and that Jesus was the incarnation of the undivided Godhead.[4]

In the view of prominent church historians such as Adolph Harnack, modalism was once the majority view and was the most significant rival to trinitarianism from about A.D. 180 to 300.[5] Although "the process is quite in obscurity,"[6] by the end of the third century it appears that church leaders had mostly rejected modalism in favor of making a personal distinction between God the Father and Jesus Christ.

The nature of this distinction was not clear, however. The Greek Apologists, prominent Christian philosophical writers in the second century, had spoken of Jesus primarily as the Logos (Word). By and large, they viewed the Logos as a second divine person subordinate to the Father. They called both persons God, but they did not view the Logos as coequal or coeternal with the Father.

Tertullian and Origen were leading opinion makers in the third century whom the institutional church nevertheless ultimately condemned as heretics. They argued in favor of a trinity of persons in the Godhead, but they too subordinated Jesus to the Father. They moved closer to the later trinitarian formulation, however—Tertullian by emphasizing that the three persons were of one substance and Origen by introducing the doctrine that the Father and Son were coeternal.

Around 318 a controversy erupted in Alexandria, Egypt, over the nature of the second person. The conflict arose over the teachings of Arius (280?-336), a presbyter (preacher) in Alexandria, who derived much of his thinking from his teacher, Lucian of Antioch.

Like the Christians of earlier times, Arius emphasized the absolute oneness of God, using biblical passages such as Deuteronomy 6:4, and he therefore rejected the trinitarian thinking that was becoming predominant. Like the trinitarians, however, he used a threefold baptismal formula and believed that Jesus was a second person called the Logos or Son. His way of reconciling these conflicting views was to deny that Jesus was God. He held, in the words of Louis Berkhof, that the Son was "created out of nothing before the world was called into being, and for that very reason was not eternal nor of the divine essence."[7] To Arius Jesus was the first and most exalted created being; the supreme agent of God; in effect, a demigod. Jehovah's Witnesses today espouse essentially the same view.

Arius's view was similar to that of the Greek Apologists of the second century and to that of the dynamic monarchians, a dissident group in the third century. It was a logical extension of the idea of subordination that was inherent in trinitarianism thus far, for it acknowledged that Jesus was divine but not deity.

While Arius was devoted to monotheism, he vehemently opposed modalism (Sabellianism), and "he protested against what he believed to be the Sabellianism of his bishop, Alexander."[8] He objected to Alexander's stress on the deity of Christ, although Alexander was actually a trinitarian rather than a modalist.

The immediate cause of the contention between them was Arius's interpretation of Proverbs 8:22-31, a passage that personifies wisdom as an attribute of God. Beginning with the second-century Apologists, theologians commonly identified wisdom in Proverbs as a second divine person, the Son-Logos. Verse 22 says, "The LORD possessed me in the beginning of his way, before his works

11

of old." Since the Hebrew word translated as "possessed" can mean "created" or "brought forth," Arius interpreted the passage to mean that God created the Son at a certain point in time before the creation of the world.

Alexander called a synod in Alexandria, which excommunicated Arius and his friends in 321. Arius obtained the support of Bishop Eusebius of Nicomedia, however, and continued the controversy. Both Alexander and Arius enlisted a number of bishops to their respective sides, and the dispute threatened to disrupt the Christian church throughout the Roman Empire.

News of the controversy reached Emperor Constantine, who had little interest in or understanding of the crucial theological issue at stake—the deity of Jesus—but was concerned that the dispute could cause division in his empire. Constantine had long realized that paganism was dying and that only Christianity could provide the religious, cultural, and philosophical unity his diverse empire needed. In 313, after he defeated his rival Maxentius in 312, he and his coemperor Licinius granted freedom of worship to Christians. In 324 he defeated Licinius and became the sole Roman emperor, and that same year he publicly embraced Christianity. He delayed his baptism as a Christian until shortly before his death in 337, however, on the theory that he could continue to sin and then receive remission of sins in the end. As an example of his morals, in 326 he executed his son, nephew, and wife for reasons that are unclear.

Will Durant explained Constantine's political interests:

He cared little for the theological differences that

agitated Christendom—though he was willing to suppress dissent in the interests of imperial unity. Throughout his reign he treated the bishops as his political aides; he summoned them, presided over their councils, and agreed to enforce whatever opinion their majority should formulate. . . . Christianity was to him a means, not an end.[9]

Walter Nigg similarly concluded, "Constantine . . . treated religious questions solely from a political point of view."[10]

Initially, Constantine sought to resolve the dispute between Arius and Alexander by appealing to both parties to forgive one another and to seek peace and unanimity. He told them the controversy was "of a truly insignificant character, and quite unworthy of such fierce contention" and "an unprofitable question" that "was wrong in the first instance to propose" and that was on "subjects so sublime and abstruse."[11]

Eventually he realized that the problem could not be resolved so easily. At the urging of his close advisor, Bishop Hosius of Cordova, he summoned the first ecumenical council of postapostolic Christendom to deal with the matter and paid the expenses for the delegates.

2

The Council of Nicea

The council convened in 325 in Nicea (also known as Nicaea and Nice; now Isnik, Turkey), a crossroads of commerce in Bithynia (northwest Asia Minor) twenty miles from the imperial court in Nicomedia. Around 250 or 300 bishops attended,[12] about one-sixth of the total number in Christendom, and almost all of them were from the Greek-speaking lands bordering the eastern Mediterranean. Only seven Western delegates attended, including two representatives from the bishop of Rome, who was not present. Each bishop had several people in his entourage, so the total number in attendance was approximately fifteen hundred to two thousand. The council lasted about six weeks.

Constantine opened the council as the honorary presiding officer, and his advisor Hosius, the most prominent Western delegate, served as chairman. Bishop Eusebius of Caesarea sat at the emperor's right hand, a position of honor.

Three factions soon became apparent. First there were the Homoousians, a minority led by Alexander of Alexandria and Athanasius (300?-373), his aide and later his successor as bishop. Although Athanasius was a young man (about 25) and of low ecclesiastical rank (archdeacon), he became the champion of this party because of his brilliance, eloquence, and decisive leadership in the post-Nicene era. The Homoousians argued that the Father and the Son were *homoousios,* or "of the same substance," and to support this view Alexander and Athanasius advocated the eternal generation of the Son as taught by Origen.

A second faction was the Arian minority, led by Bishop Eusebius of Nicomedia and Arius. Eusebius proposed an Arian creed, signed by eighteen bishops, that the council immediately rejected. The Arians found support in some statements of Origen indicating that the Son was of a different substance from the Father.

The third group, the majority, did not fully understand the issues but wanted peace. In general, they took an intermediate position, but it is difficult to characterize them as a whole. Philip Schaff explained, "Many of them had an orthodox instinct, but little discernment; others were disciples of Origen, or preferred simple biblical expression to a scholastic terminology; others had no firm convictions, but only uncertain opinions."[13] Many of them were reluctant to condemn Arius or adopt the Homoousian position. Many seemed to embrace both strands of Origen's teaching: that the Son was a second eternal person in the Deity and that the Son was subordinate to the Father. Because of these views, historians sometimes characterize many in this group as Semi-Arians or Origenists.

Bishop Eusebius of Caesarea, a leader of this third group, proposed a compromise creed used as a baptismal confession in his city. It simply said that Jesus is "the

Word of God, God of God, . . . the first-born of all creatures, begotten of the Father before all time."[14] Most of
the bishops were happy with this formula, Constantine
approved it, and the Arians were willing to subscribe to
it, but Alexander and Athanasius objected strongly, for
it did not resolve the issue at hand.

Finally, Constantine, wishing to obtain the most
unanimous decision possible and evidently prompted by
Hosius, advocated inclusion of the key word: *homoousios.*
This term had a checkered history. It originated with the
Gnostic Valentine, quoted by Irenaeus. Origen used it in
a trinitarian manner, while some Sabellians used it against
trinitarianism. At a synod in Antioch in 264 that deposed
Paul of Samosata, a dynamic monarchian, followers of
Origen condemned this word because of its use by Paul.[15]

The word was unacceptable to the Arians. The Origenists were also uncomfortable with it, because to them
it implied Sabellianism, namely, that as to His deity Jesus
was actually the Father Himself.[16] Some of them proposed
instead the word *homoiousios,* roughly meaning "of like
substance." The difference between the two positions was
literally one *iota,* one Greek letter.

In the end, the position of Athanasius prevailed.
Hosius announced a modified version of Eusebius of
Caesarea's creed that included the language required by
the Athanasian party, and the council adopted it. Otto
Heick concluded of Athanasius, "At Nicea his eloquence
was so convincing that the small minority of the Homoou-
sians prevailed over the large and influential majority of
Arians and Semi-Arians."[17]

The intervention of Constantine was also decisive.
According to Berkhof, "after considerable debate the

emperor finally threw the weight of his authority into the balance and thus secured the victory for the party of Athanasius.''[18]

Constantine enforced the decision of the council by threatening to banish all dissenters. In the end, only Arius and two bishops refused to sign the creed passed by the council, and they went into exile. Two other bishops, including Eusebius of Nicomedia, refused to sign the attached condemnatory clause and were deposed. But as Jaroslav Pelikan, author of the most comprehensive church history in the twentieth century, observed, "All the rest saluted the emperor, signed the formula, and went right on teaching as they always had. In the case of most of them, this meant a doctrine of Christ somewhere between that of Arius and that of Alexander."[19]

The council also decided upon various matters of church and clergy discipline and established a uniform method to determine the date for Easter. Some bishops proposed a rule of celibacy for all preachers, including married men. The council decided that men who married before they entered the ministry could continue to live with their wives, but unmarried men were not to marry after ordination.

The Council of Nicea is of immense historical significance as (1) the first ecumenical council of postapostolic Christendom, (2) the first (but not final) official step in the formulation of orthodox trinitarianism, and (3) the prime development in the merger of church and state. The Roman emperor pronounced the decrees of the council to be divinely inspired, promulgated them as laws of the empire, and made disobedience punishable by death. For the first time a political ruler convened an ecclesiastical council, became a decisive factor in determining doctrine, and instituted a church creed. For the first time Christendom adopted a written creed other than Scripture and made subscription to it mandatory. And for the first time the state inflicted civil penalties on people who did not conform to church dogma.

3

The Original Nicene Formulation

Because of its historical significance, it is important to examine what the Council of Nicea actually passed. It was not the Nicene Creed in use today. The original Nicene formula stated:

We believe in one God, the Father Almighty, Maker of all things visible and invisible.

And in one Lord Jesus Christ, the Son of God, begotten of the Father, the only begotten; that is, of the essence of the Father, God of God, Light of Light, very God of very God, begotten, not made, being of one substance with the Father; by whom all things were made both in heaven and on earth; who for us men, and for our salvation, came down and was incarnate and was made man; he suffered, and the third day he rose again, ascended into heaven; from thence he shall come to judge the quick and the dead.

And in the Holy Ghost.

But those who say: "There was a time when he was not"; and "He was not before he was made"; and

"He was made out of nothing," or "He is of another substance" or "essence," or "The Son of God is created," or "changeable," or "alterable"—they are condemned by the holy catholic and apostolic church.[20]

While this confession was threefold, it was not explicitly trinitarian, for it did not state that Father, Son, and Holy Ghost were three distinct persons. Rather, its fundamental purpose was to affirm the deity of Jesus Christ against the Arians. The words "of the essence of the Father" *(ek tes ousias tou patros)* and "of one substance with the Father" *(homoousion to patri)* clearly refute Arianism, and the condemnatory clause pronounces an anathema on various Arian formulations.

This creed did not take a clear position relative to modalism, however, for its key phrases allowed a Sabellian interpretation. While Athanasius himself did not mean them in a Sabellian sense, many signers had reservations about the creed precisely because it seemed too Sabellian. While there was no organized Sabellian party at the council, it is plausible that some bishops who adhered to the creed were essentially modalistic in their thinking. As Archibald Robertson noted in *The Nicene and Post-Nicene Fathers,* the Council of Nicea did not clearly distinguish itself from modalism.[21]

The phrase "God of God . . . very God of very God" may imply two divine persons, but it can also be understood as simply referring to the Incarnation. From a Oneness perspective, perhaps the most questionable phrase is the anathema on those who say the "Son of God" is "changeable" or "alterable," since it implies the doc-

22

trine of the eternal Son. Modalists and Oneness believers would agree that "the Word" or "the deity of Jesus" is not changeable or alterable, which is the intent of the statement, but technically they would argue that "the Son" has reference to the Incarnation and so had a beginning.[22] Since this phrase was not part of the creed itself, since it strongly affirms the deity of Jesus, and since its intent was to condemn the Arian position, a modalistic thinker at the council probably would have had little difficulty with it.

Ironically, another phrase in the same anathema does not harmonize with modern trinitarianism. It condemns those who say the Son is of another "substance" or "essence," using two Greek words that were basically synonymous at the time: *hypostasis* and *ousia*. But as we shall see, the official trinitarian formulation of the late fourth century is "one *ousia* (substance) and three *hypostases* (persons)." Of course, the participants at Nicea did not use these terms in their later technical sense, but if the terminology of the Nicene formula is inconsistent with modern Oneness it is also inconsistent with modern trinitarianism.

4

Post-Nicene Controversy

In hindsight, Nicea was a watershed of history, but at the time it did not settle anything. The Arian controversy continued unabated; in fact, it intensified. The next fifty years were a seesaw battle between the Athanasians and Arians, and during much of this time the Arians seemed to prevail. Political, ecclesiastical, and theological factors were all integral parts of the controversy and its ultimate outcome.

In the political arena, the Arians convinced Constantine to reopen the issue. Arius sent the emperor a conciliatory letter with an ambiguous confession of faith that satisfied him. At Constantine's behest, another council in Nicea in 327 pronounced Arius and Eusebius of Nicomedia to be orthodox. By 328 Eusebius of Nicomedia was back from exile and was one of the emperor's counselors. In fact, it was the Arian bishop Eusebius who baptized Constantine in 337.

Constantine convened a council in Tyre in 335 that reversed the Council of Nicea, deposed Athanasius (who had become bishop of Alexandria in 328), sent him into exile, and reinstated Arius. Eusebius of Caesarea played a leading role at this council; according to Epiphanius he presided over it. The night before Arius was to be officially accepted into communion at the church in Constantinople, he died at age eighty of an attack like cholera while attending a call of nature. Athanasius considered this event to be the judgment of God and circulated a gruesome story about the manner of his death, comparing it to that of Judas.

When Constantine died in 337, his three sons succeeded him, and they permitted the exiled bishops, including Athanasius, to return. In the West, Constantine II and Constans followed the Nicene doctrine, which prevailed there; in the East, Constantius was a strong advocate of Arianism, which prevailed there.

In 339 Eusebius of Nicomedia became bishop of Constantinople, the imperial capital, and Arians dominated the city for the next forty years. Athanasius was deposed a second time and fled to Rome, whose bishop supported him.

Bishop was pitted against bishop, council against council, creed against creed. Clashes between rival factions frequently resulted in bloodshed. For example, three thousand people died in a riot in Constantinople over the imperial appointment of an Arian bishop. Will Durant commented, "Probably more Christians were slaughtered by Christians in . . . two years (342-3) than by all the persecutions of Christians by pagans in the history of Rome."[23]

In 353 Constantius became the sole ruler, his two brothers having been eliminated in war, and the empire became officially Arian. Athanasius was exiled once again, and under duress the aged Hosius signed an Arian creed. Liberius, bishop of Rome, was deposed and replaced by

Felix II, an Arian. Liberius signed an Arian creed to regain his position but later returned to the Nicene view.

The victorious Arians soon split into factions, which proved to be their undoing. The extremists followed the logical implications of Arius's own position and said that Christ was "of a different substance" (*heterousios*) from the Father or "unlike" (*anomoios*) the Father—fallible and capable of sin. The majority said He was "like" (*homois*) the Father. Some were willing to say that Christ was *homoiousios* with the Father, meaning "of similar substance" or "like in every respect." They are sometimes called Semi-Arians, but Athanasius perceived that actually they were closer to the Nicene position than to Arianism, and he made conciliatory overtures toward them. The doctrinal formulation of the three Cappadocians provided a basis for agreement, and although Athanasius died in 373, the resulting alliance led to the ultimate triumph of his basic views at the Council of Constantinople in 381.

5

The Role of Athanasius

Historians give much credit for the victory of the Nicene position to Athanasius personally. He was exiled no less than five times, but he remained steadfast in his convictions. Citing his firmness throughout all the theological battles, Durant said, "To him, above all, the Church owes her doctrine of the Trinity."[24] Likewise, Heick stated, "The decisive factor in the victory of homoousianism was the unfaltering determination of Athanasius during a long life of persecution and oppression."[25]

Athanasius presented four major arguments for the true deity of Christ. First, the Scriptures clearly teach the deity of Jesus. Some of his favorite proofs were John 10:30; 14:9; 14:10. Second, Christians have always worshiped Jesus. Third, the plan of salvation requires it. Only if Jesus is truly God can He save us. Only if He is both God and man can He unite humanity to God. Finally, Athanasius used Greek philosophy to argue that the Logos must participate in the essence of God.

To counter Arian arguments from Scripture that Christ was inferior to the Father, Athanasius consistently said these biblical examples—such as Christ's prayer at Gethsemane and His statement that the Son did not know all things—related only to the humanity of Christ, not to the Godhead. He interpreted the key Arian text, Proverbs 8:22, as a reference to the preordained plan for the Incarnation: "It is true to say that the Son was created too, but this took place when He became man; for creation belongs to man."[26] He explained that when the Bible says Christ is at the right hand of the Father it means "that the Godhead of the Father is the same as the Son's," and in this sense the Father is on the Son's right hand too. "The Son reigns in His Father's kingdom, is seated upon the same throne as the Father, and is contemplated in the Father's Godhead."[27]

Athanasius said, "The Father's deity passes into the Son without flow and without division."[28] Moreover, "the fulness of the Father's Godhead is the Being of the Son, and the Son is whole God. . . . The Godhead of the Son is the Father's, and it is in the Son . . . for in the Son is contemplated the Father's Godhead."[29]

In a modalistic analogy, he compared the Father and Son to the Roman emperor and the image of the emperor. Just as to worship the image of the emperor is to worship the emperor himself, so to worship the Son is to worship the Father, for the Son is the Father's image. Similarly, he compared the Father and the Son to light and radiance from the light.

On the other hand, Athanasius insisted on differentiating the three persons, and based on Matthew 28:19, he advocated a threefold baptismal formula. In distinguishing the Father from the Son, he compared them to a well and a river produced from the well. The same water is present in both, but the well is not the river, nor is the river the well. They are not separate, yet they are two visible objects, and they have two names.

The main concern of Athanasius was to vindicate the deity of Jesus Christ. He believed the Father and the Son to be distinct persons, but he was unable to articulate the distinction satisfactorily to his opponents because of his exaltation of Christ.

6

The Role of Modalism

Although by the end of the third century modalism was no longer generally accepted, it still loomed large in the fourth-century debates. By this time theologians had only a superficial understanding of modalism. Athanasius, for example, thought that he could refute Sabellianism simply by proving the humanity of Christ and showing that He was the Son.[30] Although Athanasius denounced Sabellianism, his opponents, both at Nicea and later, objected that his formulation advocated Sabellianism. This charge is perhaps the major reason the Arians were so successful in igniting such great controversy after Nicea.[31]

In fact, some members of the Nicene party apparently were modalists, which lent credence to the accusations of the Arians and Semi-Arians. A synod at Antioch in 330 deposed Eustathius, bishop of Antioch, on charges of Sabellianism, and a synod at Constantinople in 336 deposed Marcellus, bishop of Ancyra, on the same charges. Both men were staunch opponents of Arianism, personal friends of Athanasius, and leading Homoousians at the Council of Nicea.

We cannot be certain of the true views of Eustathius,

but it appears that he and many Christians in Antioch were indeed modalistic in their beliefs.[32] He attacked the teachings of Origen, Arius, and Eusebius of Caesarea.

Marcellus clearly did advocate modalistic views. He strongly affirmed monotheism, held that the Logos was not a distinct person but was eternally immanent in God, rejected the eternal generation of the Son, taught that the term *Son* referred only to the Incarnation, and said the Father was in Christ.[33] Archibald Robertson described him as "a representative of the traditional theology of Asia Minor, as we find it in Ignatius and Irenaeus, . . . [holding to] an archaic conservatism akin to the 'naive modalism' of the early Church."[34] His pupil Photinus, bishop of Sirmium, veered in the direction of dynamic monarchianism, however, speaking of Christ as a man deified by the indwelling Logos.

Athanasius vigorously defended both Eustathius and Marcellus.[35] To him, all those who opposed Arius were supporters of the Nicene position.[36] Julius, bishop of Rome, supported both Athanasius and Marcellus, harboring them during their exile together. A council in Sardica (modern Sofia, Bulgaria) in 343 pronounced Marcellus to be orthodox.

According to Hilary, however, Athanasius finally spoke against Marcellus. Athanasius also reported that a council at Sirmium in 351 pronounced anathemas on the following modalistic views: the Son is before Mary only according to foreknowledge; the Son is the mental or pronounced Word of God; in Genesis 1:26 God was speaking to Himself instead of to the Son; Jacob wrestled with the ingenerate God instead of the Son; Genesis 19:24 does not speak of the Father and the Son; the

Father, Son, and Holy Ghost are one person; and the Holy Ghost is the ingenerate God.[37] One tradition says that in his old age Marcellus confessed the eternal trinity and the preexistent, personal Son.[38]

The *Fourth Oration against the Arians* by Pseudo-Athanasius seeks to refute modalistic views, apparently those held by Marcellus and his followers.[39] It speaks against those who use John 10:30 to teach "the two things are one, or that the one has two names" (9). It records three views against the doctrine of the eternal Son: "Some say the man whom the Saviour assumed is the Son; and others both that the man and the Word then became the Son, when they were united. And others say that the Word Himself then became Son when He became man" (15). The author affirmed that the Word is the eternal Son and denied that God is Father, Son, and Holy Ghost only in the sense of operating in different roles (25).

Eusebius of Caesarea, a leading Semi-Arian after the Council of Nicea, the first church historian, and the flattering biographer of Constantine, was motivated by a strong anti-Sabellianism. In explaining Eusebius's opposition to Athanasius, Arthur Cushman stated:

> Sabellianism was in the beginning and remained throughout his life the heresy which he most dreaded, and which he had perhaps most reason to dread. He must, even at the Council of Nicaea, have suspected Athanasius, who laid so much stress upon the unity of essence on the part of Father and Son, of a leaning toward Sabellianistic principles; and this suspicion must have been increased when he discovered, as he believed, that Athanasius' most staunch supporter, Eustathius, was a genuine Sabellian.[40]

Although Eusebius signed the Nicene formula, he interpreted it contrary to its intent. He held that "of one substance with the Father" meant "the Son was from the Father, not however a part of his essence . . . that the Son of God bears no resemblance to the originated creatures, but that to His Father alone who begat Him is He in every way assimilated. . . . [The Son] was of an essence . . . generated from the Father."[41] He spoke of "two essences," saying Jesus had a "second essence" and was "another God," a "second God," and a "second Lord."[42]

Not long before the Council of Constantinople in 381, Basil, bishop of Caesarea, spoke of a revival of Sabellianism.[43] Canon 7 of that council confirmed the existence of many modalists in its day and rejected their baptism. Significantly, Basil acknowledged that some modalists appealed to the language of the Council of Nicea to support their views.[44]

Basil denounced Sabellius as an atheist, a heretic, and insane. As we shall see, he defended trinitarian baptism by appealing to Matthew 28:19, and he rejected the idea that this verse referred to one name rather than three. It is likely that he was responding to people who baptized in the name of Jesus Christ.

Clearly, then, some people in the fourth century held modalistic views. They were some of the most vigorous opponents of Arianism, and as a result they originally allied themselves with the Athanasian party. This association with modalism, sometimes only perceived and sometimes real, caused the Semi-Arians to attack the Nicene formula. Eventually, however, the Athanasians were able to triumph by winning the Semi-Arians to their side, and people with modalistic ideas were isolated and rejected.

7

The Debate over the Holy Spirit

The debate over the Father and the Son eventually extended to the Holy Spirit. For most of the fourth century, the status of the Holy Spirit was unclear in the minds of many. As late as 380 Gregory of Nazianzus wrote that among the defenders of Nicea "some have conceived of him as an activity, some as a creature, some as God; and some have been uncertain which to call him."[45] The Arians spoke of three divine persons, citing Matthew 28:19, but to them only the Father was God, and the Son and Spirit were lesser created beings. Macedonius, bishop of Constantinople, similarly taught that the Spirit was a subordinate creature, and he had many followers.

Athanasius was the first theologian to devote extensive attention to the Holy Spirit as a distinct person, and so the first to develop a truly trinitarian theology. He used Matthew 28:19 to support his view.

The three Cappadocians were also powerful champions of the distinct personality and deity of the Holy Spirit. Gregory of Nazianzus claimed that the deity of the Holy Spirit was originally hidden from the disciples but

37

gradually revealed to the church. Citing John 16:12-13, he noted that the Lord could not teach everything to His disciples but promised that the Holy Spirit would guide them into all truth. According to Gregory, one of the truths that the Holy Spirit subsequently revealed was the Spirit's own personality and deity.[46]

The Cappadocians' definition of the trinity eventually carried the day in the controversies over both the Son and the Spirit. Let us now turn to an examination of their views.

8

The Cappadocian Formulation

The province of Cappadocia in Asia Minor produced three prominent theologians born after Nicea who crafted the trinitarian dogma that ultimately prevailed: Basil (330?-79), bishop of Caesarea; his younger brother Gregory (335?-94), bishop of Nyssa; and their close friend, Gregory of Nazianzus (died 390), who served for a short time as bishop of Constantinople. With the aid of prevalent Greek philosophical concepts, they refined the terminology of Athanasian trinitarianism to make it broadly acceptable. Their doctrinal synthesis is the basis of trinitarianism today.

The key to their formulation was a distinction between person and substance. The Greek philosopher Plato had taught that everything in the physical world was a particular instance of an intangible ideal, form, or universal in the world of ideas, which was the real world. Thus each person was an individual expression of the eternal, changeless ideal of humanity.

The Cappadocians applied this concept to the Godhead by making a distinction between two hitherto synonymous Greek words, *hypostasis* and *ousia,* which meant being, substance, or essence. They explained that the Godhead consisted of one essence or substance (*ousia*) but subsisted in three individualized particularizations (*hypostases*). The equivalent Latin formula was one *substantia* and three *personae,* terminology Tertullian had coined in the third century. In English it became one *substance* and three *persons.* As an alternative, the Cappadocians allowed the use of *prosopon* for person, but this term was not as attractive, since it originally meant face, countenance, or mask, and Sabellius had used it to mean manifestation or role.

The Cappadocian formula overcame the reluctance of many people who disliked *homoousios* ("same substance") because it sounded Sabellian. Athanasius had tried to allay the fears of these Semi-Arians by labeling the Sabellian view as *monoousios* ("one substance"), but this terminology seemed to make a distinction without a difference. To the end Athanasius stubbornly held on to the language of Nicea, which equated *ousia* and *hypostasis.* He argued that three *prosopa* did not make enough of a distinction but three *hypostases* made too great of a distinction. After all, the Arians were fond of speaking of three *hypostases,* and against them the Council of Nicea had said the Father and Son had the same *hypostasis.*

Eventually Athanasius reluctantly agreed that the Cappadocians' formula was acceptable. He presided over a council in Alexandria in 362 that condemned both Sabellianism and Arianism, advocated the use of the older Nicene language, but also acknowledged that the language of three *hypostases* was orthodox. Commenting on this council, Gregory of Nazianzus explained:

We use in an orthodox sense the terms one Essence

and three Hypostases, the one to denote the nature of the Godhead, the other the properties of the Three; the Italians mean the same, but, owing to the scantiness of their vocabulary, and its poverty of terms, they are unable to distinguish between Essence and Hypostases, and therefore introduce the term Persons [*prosopa*], to avoid being understood to assert three Essences. . . . Sabellianism was suspected in the doctrine of Three Persons, Arianism in that of Three Hypostases. . . . [Athanasius] found that they had the same sense, and . . . by permitting each party to use its own terms, he bound them together in unity of action.[47]

While the Cappadocian formulation gained support from both Athanasians and Semi-Arians, it faced some "quasi-Sabellian resistance to the notion of distinct hypostases." It "effectively removed the taint of Sabellianism from the Nicene confession, but it did so by raising another specter . . . the threat of tritheism. . . . The monotheistic confession of Deuteronomy 6:4 . . . seemed to be at stake once more."[48]

Opponents of the Cappadocians denounced them as believers in three gods, but they denied the charge. For all practical purposes, however, their view is indistinguishable from tritheism. Athanasius set the stage for this problem by speaking of all men as having the same substance (*homoousios*). The Cappadocians followed this implication and consistently compared the Godhead to three men: just as Peter, James, and John were three persons who had the same human nature, so the Father, Son, and Holy Spirit were three persons who had the same divine nature.[49] Tony Lane observed:

Their explanation lays them open to the charge of tritheism (belief in three Gods). If the relation between the common substance of the Godhead and the individual hypostases is like that between humanity and individual people, then surely there must be three Gods? The problem is compounded by the fact that the comparison with three people is no mere passing analogy. Basil offers it as part of his *definition* of the terms substance and hypostasis.[50]

In trying to answer this objection, Gregory of Nyssa admitted, "The question is . . . very difficult to deal with." He proceeded to explain that the term "many men" is a customary abuse of language, which everyone understands to refer to one nature, not many, but since the term "three gods" implies three different natures it would be wrong to use. For technical accuracy, he said, we ought to speak of "one man" and "one God." He also noted that, unlike three men, the members of the trinity always participate in each other's work. "Every operation which extends from God to the Creation . . . has its origin from the Father, and proceeds through the Son, and is perfected in the Holy Ghost."[51]

Renowned doctrinal historian Reinhold Seeberg noted the change of emphasis from Athanasius to the Cappadocians:

The modification which has been made in the ancient Nicene doctrine is very evident. Athanasius (and Marcellus) taught that there is the one God, leading a threefold personal life, who reveals Himself as such. The Cappadocians thought of three divine hypostases which, as they manifest the same dignity, are recognized as possessing one nature and the same dignity. . . . The Cappadocians interpreted the doctrine of Athanasius in accordance with the conceptions and underlying principles of the Logos-Christology of Origen. They paid a high price for their achievement, the magnitude of which they did not realize—the idea of the personal God. Three personalities and an abstract, impersonal essence resulted. . . . Thus, in place of the conception of the one-natured, threefold God had come the doctrine of the like-natured, triune God.[52]

Although the Cappadocians affirmed the coequality of persons in the Godhead, they did not totally divest themselves of subordinationistic ideas carried over from third-century trinitarianism. To retain a personal concept of God despite the impersonal essence that their theory called for, they identified the Father as the source, origin, and commander in the Godhead.

Again, the problem had already surfaced with Athanasius. He compared the Father and Son to a well and a river produced from it, saying, "So the Father's deity passes into the Son."[53] He also recorded that a council at Sirmium said Christ was true God yet "subordinate to the Father."[54]

In the writings of the Cappadocians this subordination of Jesus and the Spirit is prominent. Basil taught, "You are therefore to perceive three, the Lord who gives the order, the Word who creates, and the Spirit who confirms," and "the natural Goodness and the inherent Holiness and the royal Dignity extend from the Father through the Only-begotten to the Spirit," and the Father is the "origin of God."[55]

Gregory of Nyssa wrote, "Grace flows down in an unbroken stream from the Father, through the Son and the Spirit, upon the persons worthy of it." "The idea of cause differentiates the Persons of the Holy Trinity": "One is the Cause, and another is of the Cause. . . . One is directly from the first Cause, and another by that which is directly from the first Cause."[56]

Gregory of Nazianzus went so far as to say, "I should like to call the Father the greater, because from him flows both the Equality and the Being of the Equals (this will be granted on all hands), but I am afraid to use the word Origin, lest I should make Him the Origin of Inferiors. . . . The word Greater . . . does not apply to the Nature, but only to Originator."[57]

Like Athanasius, the Cappadocians answered Arian arguments from Scripture about the inferiority of the Son by saying these passages related to His manhood. So Basil handled Proverbs 8:22; Matthew 28:18; John 14:28; 17:5; Philippians 2:9; I Corinthians 15:28; and so Gregory of Nazianzus explained Matthew 27:46; Mark 13:32; Luke 22:42; I Timothy 2:5.[58]

While this response was an effective and accurate way to refute Arianism, it undercuts the personal distinction between Father and Son as well as the use of these passages by trinitarian apologists against Oneness believers today. For example, Gregory said concerning Christ's prayer in Luke 22:42 that the Godhead has one will common to all the persons, while trinitarians today often try to prove two persons in this passage by claiming it alludes to two divine wills.

44

Opponents of the Cappadocians argued that the Scriptures did not use their terminology and even contradicted it. They cited Hebrews 1:3, which says the Son is the express image of God's one *hypostasis,* not a second *hypostasis.* Basil responded that Hebrews 1:3 did not deny a plurality of persons but only showed the relationship of the Son to the Father. In other words, when we gaze on the Son we become aware of the Father also.[59]

Basil also answered the objection that the apostles baptized only in the name of Jesus. He argued that some passages mentioned baptism in the name of Jesus while others mentioned the baptism of the Holy Spirit, but both were an abbreviated reference to the same thing: baptism in the names of the three persons.[60] He insisted that Matthew 28:19 referred to three names, not one, and that the supreme name of Acts 4:12 was "Son of God."[61]

In sum, the Cappadocians taught that the one Godhead subsists in three coequal, coeternal, coessential persons, and this truth is an incomprehensible mystery. There is communion of substance but distinction of personhood. This trinity is a perfect, inseparable, indivisible union, and the persons work together in all things. The unique distinguishing characteristics of the persons are as follows: the Father is unbegotten, the Son is begotten (generated), and the Holy Spirit is proceeding (spirated). The generation of the Son and the procession of the Holy Spirit are mysteries, however. While the persons are coequal and coeternal, the Father is in some sense the head and the origin.[62]

Much of this formulation sounds like Orwellian doublespeak with no objective meaning. For example, if the only clear distinctions among the three persons are generation and procession, and if these processes are incomprehensible to us, then in what meaningful way can we speak or even think of God as being three persons? Pelikan has accurately commented on the confusion and evasion:

> This puzzling, indeed frustrating, combination of philosophical terminology for the relation of One and Three with a refusal to go all the way toward a genuinely speculative solution was simultaneously typical of the theology of the Cappadocians and normative for the subsequent history of trinitarian doctrine. . . . Basil's answer to . . . difficult[ies] was to declare that what was common to the Three and what was distinctive among them lay beyond speech and comprehension and therefore beyond either analysis or conceptualization.[63]

Another trinitarian scholar, Harold O. J. Brown, has similarly described the vagueness, ambiguity, and philosophical speculation inherent in the Cappadocians' doctrine:

> The language was so abstract and intangible that it did not really help believers to form a clear picture of what each of the three Persons is like. By its abstraction, the Cappadocian theology seems fairly far removed from the dynamic process by which the Christian community first achieved the conviction of the deity of Christ. . . . Trinitarianism seems to replace living faith with metaphysical dogmatics.[64]

In elaborating on these problems, Brown quoted Seeberg,

but he sought to moderate Seeberg's criticism and to offer a defense of trinitarianism:

It is not possible to observe the different Persons in action. Their distinction can only be learned from God's self-disclosure in Scripture. It lies in the internal relationships or properties of the Persons: ingenerateness, begottenness, and procession. This sounds very theoretical. Reinhold Seeberg put it caustically: "Thus one arrives at an empty metaphysics or conceptual mythology; the Father begets the Son and causes the Spirit to proceed from himself. In this way the Persons are supposed to be distinguished from one another and also united to one another." . . . To talk about properties and then say that we cannot know what they mean is exasperating. It may help to remember that the properties *explain nothing;* on the contrary, they are merely conceptual tools or symbols to impress on us that the three Persons are and remain eternally distinct, yet also remain eternally one God.[65]

This view is essentially the position of trinitarianism today.

/

9

The Council of Constantinople

The Cappadocian doctrine finally prevailed over Arianism at what is now known as the second ecumenical council. Emperor Theodosius, a Westerner who staunchly affirmed the Nicene view and who became ruler of the East in 379, convened this council in the imperial capital, Constantinople, in 381. The intervention of the emperor was crucial. "As it was the imperial power which had bestowed victory upon the Nicene Faith and then upon Arianism, so now it was the imperial influence which acted decisively in favor of the Neo-Nicene faith."[66]

The council was not truly ecumenical. Only about 150 bishops participated, and none were from the West. The two Gregorys were prominent participants, Basil having died in 379. Gregory of Nazianzus presided part of the time.

Canon 1 of the council affirmed the Council of Nicea and denounced the "Eunomians [Anomians, or extreme Arians], Eudoxians [mainline Arians], Semi-Arians or Pneumatomachi [those who denied the deity of the Holy Spirit], Sabellians, Marcellians, Photinians, and Apollinarians [those who taught that Christ had an incomplete human nature]." Canon 7 specifically repudiated both

Eunomian and Sabellian baptism. Interestingly, it identified the Sabellians with Montanists and Phrygians and
stated that they were particularly numerous in Galatia.
The Montanists, who originated in Phrygia, were noted
for their emphasis on the Holy Spirit, speaking in tongues,
prophecy, and a strict lifestyle.

The synodical letter from the assembled bishops sum-
marized their decision as follows: "There is one Godhead,
Power and Substance of the Father and of the Son and
of the Holy Ghost; the dignity being equal, and the maj-
esty being equal in three perfect hypostases, i.e., three
perfect persons."[67] The emperor endorsed the council's
decisions and enforced them as law.

Tradition says the council modified the original Nicene
formula and produced the Nicene Creed in use today,
which is therefore sometimes called the Niceno-Constan-
tinopolitan Creed. Scholars have established, however,
that the present Nicene Creed actually stems from a
fourth-century baptismal creed used in Jerusalem, which
was influenced by the original creed of Nicea. "All we
know is that from about 500 this form came to be used
in place of the original Nicene Creed."[68]

The Nicene Creed used today omits the damnatory
clause of the original as well as the important words "of
the essence of the Father" and a few minor phrases. Its
most important addition is the following: "And [I believe]
in the Holy Ghost, the Lord and Giver of Life; who pro-
ceedeth from the Father [and the Son]; who with the
Father and the Son together is worshiped and glorified."
It also confesses "one Baptism for the remission of sins."[69]
The bracketed words "and the Son" make up the *filio-
que* clause, added at the Synod of Toledo in 589. The West

accepted this teaching, but the East did not; it became a major doctrinal factor in the enduring schism between the two.

The significance of the Council of Constantinople is that it marked (1) the ultimate triumph of the Athanasian doctrine of the trinity (as refined by the Cappadocians), (2) the final defeat of Arianism, (3) the establishment of the Holy Spirit as the third coequal member of the trinity, and (4) the rejection of Apollinarianism (the belief that Christ had an incomplete human nature).

10

After Constantinople

By 381, then, the doctrine of the trinity was complete—almost. In the East, John of Damascus made some refinements in the eighth century: he rejected most of the remaining elements of subordinationism, said the persons were not related to one another as three men are, and described their interrelation as "mutual interpenetration" (circumincession) without commingling.[70]

In the West, Augustine (354-430) brought greater emphasis on the unity of essence and the equality of person, saying that each person possesses the entire essence but under a different point of view. He was uncomfortable with the word *person,* for he did not think the trinity was like three human persons, who possess in common only a generic nature.

Some of his analogies suggest modalism: he compared the trinity to memory, intelligence, and will in the human spirit; to something seen, vision, and the intention of the will uniting the two; and to something in memory, the inner vision, and the will uniting the two. His last analogy was the human mind in threefold action: remembering, understanding, and loving God.

Nevertheless, Augustine continued to speak of three

persons and defended the doctrine of the trinity. One of his most famous analogies even sounds tritheistic: the trinity is like a lover, the beloved, and the love that binds the two together.

Heick described these contrasting aspects in Augustine's teaching on the Godhead:

> The persons of the Trinity are not different from one another; with respect to the entire divine substance they are identical with each other. . . . Each of the three persons is equal to the entire Trinity, and the entire Trinity is not more than one of the persons. Augustine spoke as though the essence of Being is a Person after all. Yet Augustine, in agreement with the Church's tradition, insisted on the three persons in the Trinity. How, then, was he able to do this after his previous statements on the unity? Simply by introducing the logical category of relationship. In the one God there are three forms of existence, and the one cannot be without the other. . . . There is the relation of mutual dependency among the persons. Father, Son, and Spirit behold in themselves the entire undivided unity which belongs to each of them under a different point of view, as generating, generated, or existing through spiration.[71]

The most definitive trinitarian creed is the so-called ınasian Creed, or *Symbolum Quicunque,* which ·ged during the fifth to eighth centuries, attaining al form around the end of the eighth. Athanasius, ·se, had nothing to do with it. It includes the *filio-* ıse, and like Augustine, it expressly excludes subordinationism. It also pronounces damnation upon anyone who does not accept the doctrine of the trinity according to its terms. Roman Catholics and Protestants, including many evangelicals, still use it today.

Arianism was defeated theologically by 381, but it remained a political threat in that some of the barbarian tribes successfully invading the West were Arian. That danger ended in the sixth century with the conversion of these tribes to trinitarianism.

11

Conclusions

As a matter of history, orthodox trinitarianism did not come to us from the Bible or the early postapostolic church. It did not come directly from Tertullian and Origen, the third-century heretics who first introduced key trinitarian terms and concepts, although it was erected upon their theology. Nor did it spring whole from the Council of Nicea. Rather, it developed gradually over most of the fourth century. The key figures in this process were Athanasius, the three Cappadocians, and finally the delegates to the Council of Constantinople in 381.

Scholars are unanimous in this assessment, as shown by the following statements of Protestant church historian Jaroslav Pelikan, *The New Catholic Encyclopedia,* and the *Encyclopedia of Religion and Ethics,* respectively:

> You are not entitled to the beliefs you cherish about such things as the Holy Trinity without a sense of what you owe to those who worked this out for you. To circumvent Saint Athanasius on the assumption that if you put me alone in a room with the New Testament, I will come up with the doctrine of the Trinity, is naive. . . . The dogma of the Trinity . . . was

hammered out during the third quarter of the fourth century. . . . [The key word *homoousios* was] coined by Gnostic heretics, dictated by an unbaptized emperor, jeopardized by naive defenders, but eventually vindicated by its orthodox opponents.[72]

When one does speak of an unqualified Trinitarianism, one has moved from the period of Christian origins to, say, the last quadrant of the fourth century. It was only then that what might be called the definitive Trinitarian dogma "one God in three Persons" became thoroughly assimilated into Christian life and thought. . . . The formulation "one God in three Persons" was not solidly established, certainly not fully assimilated into Christian life and its profession of faith, prior to the end of the fourth century.[73]

At first the Christian faith was not Trinitarian in the strictly ontological reference. It was not so in the apostolic and sub-apostolic ages, as reflected in the NT and other early Christian writings. Nor was it so even in the age of the Christian apologists. And even Tertullian, who founded the nomenclature of the orthodox doctrine, knew as little of an ontological Trinity as did the apologists; his is still the economic or relative conception of the Johannine and Pauline theology. So Harnack holds, and he says further that the whole history of Christological and Trinitarian dogma from Athanasius to Augustine is the history of the displacement of the Logos-conception by that of the Son, of the substitution of the immanent and absolute Trinity for the economic and relative. . . . The orthodox doctrine in its developed form is a Trinity of essence rather than of manifestation.[74]

Many Oneness believers have an inaccurate view of the Council of Nicea, because of the simplistic treatment of popular histories and the common mistake of attributing the Nicene Creed to that council. The dispute was not between trinitarianism and modalism, nor was it over the trinitarian baptismal formula: those battles had already been decided in the third century. Moreover, the Roman Catholic Church did not orchestrate the council, for it had not yet developed theologically or ecclesiastically.

At the time, Nicea was a victory for the deity of Christ; it was not a clear rejection of Oneness. Some participants could have been essentially Oneness in their thinking, and most were not trinitarian in the modern orthodox sense. Some supporters of the winning side were modalistic or were accused of being modalistic. Many opponents of Nicea as well as some supporters interpreted the original Nicene formula in a modalistic fashion. And modalists were still teaching their views and baptizing converts when trinitarianism finally triumphed at the Council of Constantinople.

When the theological heirs of Nicea finally distanced themselves from modalism, they did so at the expense of tainting their doctrine with subordinationism and tritheism, despite their denials. And those problems still beset trinitarianism today.

Many factors contributed to the eventual victory of trinitarianism in the late fourth century. Political maneuvering, both in the state and in the church, was a crucial factor. Theologically, the bottom line is this: given the philosophical, religious, and political context and given the perceived alternatives, trinitarianism seemed the best way to defend what Christians had always believed—the deity of Jesus.

But what if the majority of Christendom had not already lost the experience of repentance and the outpouring of the Spirit? What if theologians had used Scripture, not philosophy or tradition, as their primary frame of reference? What if the bishops had rejected the merger of church and state and so protected the church from pollution by pagan thought, lifestyle, and politics? What if ecclesiastical leaders in the third century had not abandoned the historic modalism of the majority of Christians? What if fourth-century theologians had received a clear exposition of modalism and thoroughly understood its tenets? Then, perhaps, fourth-century leaders could have found a more biblical way to defend the deity of Christ against the heresy of Arianism.

Indeed, prominent twentieth-century theologians have arrived at this very conclusion. Claude Welch explained their thinking, as exemplified by John Baillie, an editor of *The Library of Christian Classics,* and A. C. McGiffert:

> [Baillie] labels the assertion that the Trinity is the distinctively Christian idea of God as "seriously misleading." "What is true is that from the third century onwards the distinctively Christian idea of God began to fit itself into a trinitarian mould." This mould was adopted and adapted from Hellenistic philosophy. .

[McGiffert] recognizes that the opponents of Arianism were interested in affirming the deity of Christ in order to guarantee the uniting of man to God, but thinks that it was only the prevailing Platonic philosophy which made it necessary to maintain the deity of Christ via the theory of pre-existence and the logos doctrine. "If . . . the immanence of God, or the oneness of divine and human nature, had been recognized by the Nicene theologians, the doctrine of the Trinity would have been unnecessary; the religious interest—to find God in Christ—could then have been conserved, as it was by the modalists, without distinguishing the pre-existent Son of God from the Father."[75]

Oneness believers today do just that. Jumping back over the centuries of philosophical speculation, creedal formulation, and man-made tradition, they seek to understand what the Bible itself says about God. They have discovered that the one true God has manifested and revealed Himself in the one human person of His Son, Jesus Christ our Lord.

Notes

[1] See David K. Bernard, *Oneness and Trinity, A.D. 100-300* (Hazelwood, MO: Word Aflame Press, 1991), 165-72.

[2] Ibid., 172-73.

[3] Ibid., 129-32, 134-36, 160.

[4] Ibid., 134-36, 154-62.

[5] Adolph Harnack, *A History of Christian Thought* (London: Williams and Norgate, 1897), 3:51-54; Otto Heick, *A History of Christian Thought* (Philadelphia: Fortress Press, 1965), 1:149.

[6] Archibald Robertson, "Prolegomena," in Philip Schaff and Henry Wace, eds., *The Nicene and Post-Nicene Fathers,* 2d ser. [hereinafter *NPNF*] (Reprint, Grand Rapids: Eerdmans, 1976), 4:xxv.

[7] Louis Berkhof, *The History of Christian Doctrines* (Grand Rapids: Baker, 1937), 84.

[8] Kenneth Scott Latourette, *A History of Christianity,* rev. ed. (San Francisco: Harper & Row, 1953, 1975), 1:153.

[9] Will and Ariel Durant, *The Story of Civilization* (New York: Simon & Schuster, 1935-75), 3:658.

[10] Walter Nigg, *The Heretics* (New York: Alfred A. Knopf, 1962), 126-27.

[11] Eusebius of Caesarea, *Life of Constantine* 2:63-71, NPNF 1:516-18.

[12] Eusebius of Caesarea said over 250 bishops attended, while Athanasius and later tradition put the figure at 318. Existing records list only about 220 names.

[13] Philip Schaff, *Nicene and Post-Nicene Christianity,* vol. 3 of *History of the Christian Church,* 5th rev. ed. (1910; Reprint, Grand Rapids: Eerdmans), 628.

[14] *NPNF* 4:74; 14:3.

[15] Schaff, *History* 3:655 nn. 2, 3.

[16]See Heick 1:159-60.

[17]Ibid., 157.

[18]Berkhof, 87.

[19]Jaroslav Pelikan, *The Emergence of the Catholic Tradition (100-600)*, vol. 1 of *The Christian Tradition: A History of the Development of Doctrine* (Chicago: University of Chicago Press, 1971), 203.

[20]Philip Schaff, ed., *The Creeds of Christendom*, 6th ed., 1931 (Reprint, Grand Rapids: Baker), 1:28-29 (English), 2:60 (Greek).

[21]*NPNF* 4:xxxii-xxxiii.

[22]Some trinitarians have also made this point, including Adam Clarke, Finis Dake, and Walter Martin.

[23]Durant 4:8.

[24]Ibid.

[25]Heick 1:157.

[26]Athanasius, *Defense of the Nicene Definition* 3:13, *NPNF* 4:158-59.

[27]Idem, *Orations against the Arians* 1:13:61, *NPNF* 4:341.

[28]Idem, *Statement of Faith*, 2, *NPNF* 4:84.

[29]Idem, *Discourse against the Arians* 3:23:5, *NPNF* 4:396.

[30]Idem, *On the Opinion of Dionysius*, 5-10, 27, NPNF 4:178-79, 187.

[31]See Latourette 1:157; Archibald Robertson, "Prolegomena," in *NPNF* 4:xxxiii.

[32]Latourette 1:158; Tony Lane, *Harper's Concise Book of Christian Faith* (San Francisco: Harper and Row, 1984), 29.

[33]Basil, *Letters*, 69, *NPNF* 8:165-66; Klotsche, 67; Schaff, *History* 3:651-53.

[34]*NPNF* 4:xxxv-xxxvi.

[35]See Athanasius, *Defense against the Arians* 3:47 and *History of the Arians* 1:4, 6, *NPNF* 4:125, 271.

[36]Idem, *Defense of the Nicene Definition* 5:20, *NPNF* 4:164.

[37]Idem, *Councils of Arminium and Seleuca [On Synods]* 2:27, *NPNF* 4:465.

[38]Henry Percival, ed., *The Seven Ecumenical Councils,* vol. 14 of *NPNF,* 176.

[39]*NPNF* 4:436-443.

[40]*NPNF* 1:24.

[41]Eusebius of Caesarea, *Letter to His Diocese, NPNF* 4:75-76.

[42]*NPNF* 4:76, n. 7.

[43]Basil, *Letters,* 210, *NPNF* 8:250.

[44]Ibid., 125, *NPNF* 8:194.

[45]Gregory of Nazianzus, *Orations* 31:5, quoted in Pelikan, 213.

[46]Idem, *On the Holy Spirit,* 27, *NPNF* 7:326.

[47]Idem, *On the Great Athanasius,* 35, *NPNF* 7:274.

[48]Pelikan, 219-21.

[49]See, for example, Basil, *Letters,* 38, *NPNF* 8:137.

[50]Lane, 34.

[51]Gregory of Nyssa, *On "Not Three Gods," NPNF* 5:331-34.

[52]Heick 1:160-61, quoting Reinhold Seeberg, *Textbook of the History of Doctrines,* trans. Charles E. Hay (Philadelphia: Lutheran Pub. Soc., 1904), 1:232-33.

[53]Athanasius, *Statement of Faith,* 2, *NPNF* 4:84.

[54]Idem, *Councils of Arminium and Seleuca [On Synods]* 2:26, *NPNF* 4:463.

[55]Basil, *On the Spirit* 16:38, 47, and *Letters,* 105, *NPNF* 8:24, 29, 186.

[56]Gregory of Nyssa, *On the Holy Spirit* and *On "Not Three Gods," NPNF* 5:323, 336

[57]Gregory of Nazianzus, *Oration on Holy Baptism,* 43, *NPNF* 7:375-76. As the ruling pigs in George Orwell's *Animal Farm* ultimately proclaimed, "All animals are equal, but some animals are more equal than others" (Harmondsworth, Middlesex, England: Penguin Books, 1945), 114.

[58]*NPNF* 8:xxxviii-xli; Gregory of Nazianzus, *Fourth Theological Oration, The Second Concerning the Son,* 5-15, *NPNF* 7:311-15.

[59]Basil, *Letters,* 38, *NPNF* 8:140-41.

[60]Idem, *On the Spirit* 12:28, *NPNF* 8:18.

[61]Idem, *Letters,* 210, *NPNF* 8:250.

[62]See Basil, *On the Spirit* 16:37-38 and *Letters,* 38, NPNF 8:23-24, 137-40; Gregory of Nyssa, *On the Holy Spirit* and *On the Holy Trinity, NPNF* 5; Gregory of Nazianzus, *Third Theological Oration, On the Son* 29:3 and *Fifth Theological Oration, On the Holy Spirit,* 8-10, *NPNF* 7:301-2, 320-21.

[63]Pelikan, 223.

[64]Brown, Harold O. J., *Heresies: The Image of Christ in the Mirror of Heresy and Orthodoxy from the Apostles to the Present* (Garden City, N.Y.: Doubleday, 1984), 153-54.

[65]Ibid., 151. The quote of Reinhold Seeburg is from *Lehrbuch der Dogmengeschichte,* 4th ed. (Tubigen: Mohr, 1909), 2:295. Emphasis is original.

[66]Heick 1:163.

[67]*NPNF* 14:173, 185, 382.

[68]Heick 1:163.

[69]Schaff, *Creeds* 2:58-59.

[70]Berkhof, 91.

[71]Heick 1:164-65.

[72]Mark A. Noll, "The Doctrine Doctor," *Christianity Today,* 10 September 1990, 26; Pelikan, 210-11.

[73]*The New Catholic Encyclopedia* (1967), s.v. "Trinity, Holy."

[74]W. Fulton, "Trinity," *Encyclopedia of Religion and Ethics,* James Hastings, et al., eds. (New York: Charles Scribner's Sons, 1951), 12:461.

[75]Claude Welch, *In This Name: The Doctrine of the Trinity in Contemporary Theology* (New York: Charles Scribner's Sons, 1952), 48-49, quoting John Baillie, *The Place of Jesus Christ in Modern Theology* (1929), 185, and A. C. McGiffert, *History of Christian Thought.*

Glossary

Arianism. The doctrine of Arius (280?-336), a presbyter at Alexandria, Egypt. Arius held that there is only one God and that the Son or Word is a divine being like God but created by God. Thus Jesus is a demigod. This view was condemned at the Council of Nicea in 325 and again at the Council of Constantinople in 381.

Athanasian Creed, or *Symbolum Quicunque.* The most definitive trinitarian creed. It emerged during the fifth to eighth centuries, attaining its final form around the end of the eighth. Athanasius had nothing to do with it.

Cappadocians. Three prominent fourth-century theologians from Cappadocia (a province in Asia Minor) who crafted the trinitarian dogma that ultimately prevailed: Basil, bishop of Caesarea; his younger brother Gregory, bishop of Nyssa; and their close friend, Gregory of Nazianzus, who served for a short time as bishop of Constantinople. With the aid of prevalent Greek philosophical concepts, they refined the terminology of Athanasian trinitarianism to make it broadly acceptable. Their doctrinal synthesis is the basis of trinitarianism today.

Constantinople, Council of. Ecumenical church council in 381 that affirmed the Council of Nicea and more clearly defined orthodox trinitarianism. It particularly established that the Holy Spirit was the third coequal person.

Dynamic monarchianism. A belief in the third century that Jesus was a human being who became the Son of God by reason of the indwelling of divine wisdom, or the Logos. Apparently, the dynamic monarchians did not consider Jesus to be God in the strict sense of the word.

Greek Apologists. Writers from approximately 130 to 180 who wrote treatises in Greek defending Christianity against attacks by pagan philosophers and writers.

Homoiousios. A Greek word meaning "of like substance, of similar substance, or like in every respect." The Semi-Arians during and after the Council of Nicea preferred this word, but ultimately they accepted the term *homoousios.*

Homoousians. Supporters of the view of Alexander and Athanasius at the Counicl of Nicea. They advocated the use of the Greek word *homoousios* ("of the same substance") to describe the relation of the Father to the Son and thus to defend the deity of Jesus. Although they were a minority at the Council of Nicea, their view prevailed.

Homoousios. A Greek word meaning "of the same substance," used by Alexander and Athanasius at the Council of Nicea to defend the deity of Jesus Christ. In opposition to the Arians, they said the Father and the Son were of the same substance. Their opponents argued that the word sounded too Sabellian.

Hypostasis (plural: *hypostases*). A Greek word translated as "person." Originally it was equivalent to the Greek word *ousia,* meaning "substance, essence, or being," and it was so used by the Council of Nicea, which denounced anyone who said the Father and the Son were of a different *hypostasis.* Similarly, Hebrews 1:2 says the Son is the express image of the Father's *hypostasis,* rather than a second *hypostasis.* The Cappadocians, however, used this word to distinguish the three persons of the trinity, saying they had one *ousia* (substance) but three *hypostases* (persons). This is now the standard trinitarian formula. Athanasius preferred the language of Nicea, saying that *hypostasis* made too much of a distinction among the three persons, but he reluctantly allowed its use.

Logos. Greek term meaning "word." In John 1:1 the term refers to God Himself, particularly with reference to His mind, plan, and self-revelation. Trinitarianism equates the Logos with the Son as the second person of the trinity.

Modalism, modalistic monarchianism. A belief predominant in the third century that Father, Son, and Holy Spirit are not distinctions in God's nature or self-conscious persons, but simply *modes* (methods, manifestations) of God's activity. As a corollary, Jesus Christ is all the fullness of the Godhead, or the Father, incarnate.

Nicea, Council of. First ecumenical church council in post-apostolic Christendom, held in the town of Nicea in 325. It condemned Arianism, asserting that the Father and Son are of the same substance. It is regarded as the first official endorsement of trinitarianism, although it did not enunciate the full trinitarian doctrine.

Nicene Creed. Definitive statement of orthodox trinitarianism that stems from a fourth-century baptismal creed used in Jerusalem. It is not the original formulation of the Council of Nicea, although it was influenced by that declaration. It is closer to the statement of the Council of Constantinople in 381.

Oneness. The belief that God is absolutely one with no distinction of persons and that Jesus is the fullness of the Godhead incarnate.

Origenists. Label sometimes used for the intermediate party at the Council of Nicea, which was the majority and which is more commonly known as the Semi-Arians. Many of this group were reluctant to condemn Arius or adopt the Homoousian position. Many seemed to embrace both strands of Origen's teaching: that the Son was a second eternal person in the Deity and that the Son was subordinate to the Father.

Ousia. A Greek word meaning "substance, essence, or being" and originally equivalent to *hypostasis.* The Council of Nicea said that the Father and the Son had the same *ousia,* or *hypostasis.* The Cappadocians used *ousia* to designate the abstract nature of deity that the three persons of the trinity shared in common, while using *hypostasis* to mean what was distinctive to each person. Thus the standard trinitarian formula is "one *ousia* in three *hypostases.*"

Prosopon (plural: *prosopa*). A Greek word originally meaning "face, countenance or mask," but eventually meaning "person." Sabellius used it to refer to the Father, Son, and Holy Spirit as three manifestations or roles of the one God. The Cappadocians allowed its use for the persons of the trinity but preferred the word *hypostasis,* which became the official term. Athanasius did not like to use *prosopon* for this purpose because he felt that it did not make enough of a distinction among the persons, but on the other hand, he felt that *hypostasis* made too much of a distinction.

Sabellianism. The modalistic beliefs promoted by a third-century teacher named Sabellius. By the fourth century, little was known of the actual views of Sabellius, but it seems clear that he emphasized the oneness of God and the absolute deity of Jesus Christ, and rejected the trinitarian thinking of his day. See Modalism.

Semi-Arians. A label used for the intermediate party at the Council of Nicea, which was the majority. They were reluctant to condemn Arius. They were willing to say the Son was similar in nature (*homoiousios*) to the Father, or like the Father in every way, but were originally hesitant to say that the Son was of the same nature (*homoousios*) as the Father, for fear this statement would lead to Sabellianism. After Nicea, this group prevailed for a while, but eventually they disagreed among themselves. Most of them eventually accepted the Cappadocian formulation of the trinity.

Subordinationism. The belief that one person in the Godhead is inferior to, subject to, lesser than, or created by another person in the Godhead. This view presupposes a plurality of persons in the Godhead. The early trinitarians subordinated the Son and Spirit to the Father.

Trinitarianism. The belief that there is one God who exists in three persons: Father, Son (or Word), and Holy Ghost (or Holy Spirit). Orthodox trinitarianism today holds that the three persons are coequal, coeternal, and consubstantial (of the same substance).

Tritheism. The belief in three gods.

Word. See Logos.

Bibliography

Bainton, Roland. *Early Christianity.* Princeton, NJ: Van Nostrand, 1960.

Berkhof, Louis. *The History of Christian Doctrines.* Grand Rapids: Baker, 1937.

Bernard, David K. *Oneness and Trinity, A.D. 100-300.* Hazelwood, MO: Word Aflame Press, 1991.

_____. *The Oneness of God.* Hazelwood, MO: Word Aflame Press, 1983.

Brown, Harold O. J. *Heresies: The Image of Christ in the Mirror of Heresy and Orthodoxy from the Apostles to the Present.* Garden City, N.Y.: Doubleday, 1984.

Deferrari, Roy J., et al., eds. *The Fathers of the Church.* New York: Fathers of the Church, n.d.

Durant, Will and Ariel. *The Story of Civilization.* New York: Simon and Schuster, 1935-75.

Harnack, Adolph. *History of Dogma.* London: Williams and Norgate, 1897.

Hastings, James, ed. *Encyclopedia of Religion and Ethics.* New York: Charles Scribner's Sons, 1951.

Heick, Otto. *A History of Christian Thought.* Philadelphia: Fortress Press, 1965.

Klotsche, E. H. *The History of Christian Doctrine.* Rev. ed. Grand Rapids: Baker, 1945, 1979.

Lane, Tony. *Harper's Concise Book of Christian Faith.* San Francisco: Harper and Row, 1984.

Latourette, Kenneth Scott. *A History of Christianity.* Rev. ed. San Francisco: Harper and Row, 1953, 1975.

New Catholic Encyclopedia, The. New York: McGraw Hill, 1967.

Nigg, Walter. *The Heretics.* New York: Alfred A. Knopf, 1962.

Noll, Mark. "The Doctrine Doctor" [Jaroslav Pelikan]. *Chris-*

tianity Today. 10 September 1990.

Pelikan, Jaroslav. *The Emergence of the Catholic Tradition (100-600).* Volume 1 of *The Christian Tradition: A History of the Development of Doctrine.* Chicago: University of Chicago Press, 1971.

Random House Encyclopedia. Electronic edition. Pittsford, NY: Microlytics, Inc. with Random House, Inc., 1990.

Schaff, Philip, and Henry Wace, eds. *The Nicene and Post-Nicene Fathers.* 2d ser. Reprint. Grand Rapids: Eerdmans, 1976.

Schaff, Philip, ed. *The Creeds of Christendom.* 6th ed. 1931. Reprint. Grand Rapids: Baker.

Schaff, Philip. *Nicene and Post-Nicene Christianity.* Volume 3 of *History of the Christian Church.* 5th rev. ed. 1910. Reprint. Grand Rapids: Eerdmans.

Software Toolworks Illustrated Encyclopedia. CD-ROM version. Novato, CA: Software Toolworks with Grolier, 1990.

Welch, Claude. *In This Name: The Doctrine of the Trinity in Contemporary Theology.* New York: Charles Scribner's Sons, 1952.

Index